In the Weather of the World

ESTHA WEINER

salmonpoetry

Published in 2013 by
Salmon Poetry
Cliffs of Moher, County Clare, Ireland
Website: www.salmonpoetry.com
Email: info@salmonpoetry.com

Copyright © Estha Weiner, 2013

ISBN 978-1-908836-23-6

All rights reserved. No part of this publication may be reproduced or transmitted in any form or by any means, electronic or mechanical, including photography, recording, or any information storage or retrieval system, without permission in writing from the publisher. The book is sold subject to the condition that it shall not, by way of trade or otherwise, be lent, resold or otherwise circulated without the publisher's prior consent in any form of binding or cover other than that in which it is published and without a similar condition, including this condition, being imposed on the subsequent purchaser.

COVER ARTWORK: Photo by Phyllis Gutmann, Martin Puryear sculpture
COVER DESIGN: *Siobhán Hutson*

Printed in Ireland by Sprint Print

For Dr. Stanley Fisher and For Bill Matthews,
once and future
and For J.E.T., now

Acknowledgements

The poems in this manuscript have appeared in the following publications or anthologies:

"Two Days After" – *J Journal* – (Nominated for 2008 Pushcart Prize)

"Local Talk, Wiscasset" – *Puckerbrush Review*

"Wild Blueberries" – *Puckerbrush Review*

"New Orleans Has Collapsed" – *Hurricane Blues* (Anthology: S.E. Missouri State University Press)

"Ballad Without Borders" – *J Journal*

"On the Island of the Old Women" – *Blues For Bill: A Tribute To William Matthews* (Anthology: University of Akron Press, Akron Poetry Series, of which Estha Weiner is co-editor and contributor)

"When my poem appeared" – *Never Before: Poems About First Experiences* (Anthology: Four Way Books)

"The News, New Year's Eve, 1999" – *Rabbit Ears* (Anthology: Poets Wear Prada)

"And that has made all the difference"– *Transfiguration Begins at Home* (Tiger Bark Press – Estha Weiner)

"At the American Burger" – *New America* (Anthology: Autumn House)

Contents

I.

Home	15
On Fabulous 57th Street	16
Public Access Pier	17
The Perfect Error	18
You Can't Make This Stuff Up	19
The French Hospital	20
The Cutting Edge	22
At 5:45 P.M. in The Conservatory Garden	23
At the National Archives on Varick Street	24
Two Days After	25

II.

Coming Home	29
This young lady	30
In the Blood	31
529 Congress Street	32
The Gifts	33
Grace	34
Local Talk, Wiscasset	35
Wild Blueberries	36
It is a northern spirit	37
End of The Season Tour	38

III.

Rocky Mountain Prelude	43
Cold Spring January	44
Ritual: South Florida	45
New Orleans Quartet: *Avant et Après*	46
Elysian Fields *or* There's A Full Moon	
Over The Steamer Natchez	46
A Good Story	47

Do You Know What It Means To Miss…
   New Orleans?   49
New Orleans Has Collapsed   49

IV.

At the American Burger	53
AMERICA	54
No Problem	56
ATTENTION: DANGER BEHIND	57
Fifty years ago	58
Goodnight, David	59
And what rough beast…?	61
America Enlarges Its Vocabulary Again	62
What She Learned	63

V.

Everything Sounds So Much Better in French	67
What I Learned On My Summer Vacation	68
The Education of Crazy Jane	69
Two Testaments	70
Brigit	71
Seisun Swift, With More Than A Nod To Auden	72
THE NEWS, New Year's Eve, 1999	73
Ballad Without Borders	74

VI.

The Sign	77
One Summer Tuesday	78
Labor Day	79
Audobon Mots	80
The Problem With Nature Poetry	81
Winter	82

VII.
Loosestrife	85
On the 'Island of the Old Women,'	86
Bright Girl Wanted	87
Taking to her bed	88
My Tarot	89
The Club	90
2001	91
No Cain and Abel	92
And that has made all the difference	93
Sleep	94
Like a 'rest' in music	95
Dialogue	96
When my poem appeared	97
Sprezzatura	98

About the Author   101

A process in the weather of the heart
A process in the weather of the eye
A weather in the flesh and bone
A process in the weather of the world.

Dylan Thomas

I.

"Home"

is a restaurant
on Cornelia Street
in Greenwich Village
where you can eat
breakfast blueberry cake
like your Maine mother
used to make, when
she liked you
or even herself;
next door
a restaurant named Pearl,
for the gem
from the friction
in the oyster, where
the lobster rolls
cost something different
every day, as if
you never
left home.

On fabulous 57th Street,

a homeless woman feeds
the pigeons, who come
to eat out of her hands,
which means they have to touch her,
and when they do, she
smiles, but if they're flighty
and fly away, she clucks
her disapproval, because
she has only two bags,
one full of food for them,
because she has only
two hands, anxious
for the pecks of birds.

Public Access Pier

On the top deck
of the docked ship, free
for city summer visits,
anyone can own the river,
rock of the waves,
whisp of the white sails,
cut of the Nordic
Cruise Line, sun spread
on the water, clouds closer
than the arm of the Statue of Liberty
and the factories and fancies
of New Jersey.

The Perfect Error

She lived in a white building,
consisting of five flowers; each
flower had six apartments.

You Can't Make This Stuff Up

It was a topless bar on 43rd and Broadway,
one block from infamy –

The lights of Times Square
burned late and crazy there

Where I got a job one year
as a waitress, in a black leotard.

In this democratic hole
came Wall Street traders with a roll

Of fives they tucked up into
g-strings, but never left for tips.

A travelling salesman gave me ten bucks
for a two-buck drink, and his phone number;

The only guy who asked me for a date
was a sociologist, who came late.

A man in a tweed jacket hissed:
"What's a nice girl like you doing in a place like this?"

One dancer was so good, I wished she were in
"Chorus Line," instead of Tits and Grind.

Intoned the tough-assed waitress on my shift:
"I came here from Kansas City and I'M GONNA MAKE IT."

The French Hospital,

for a girl in love
with all of Gaul,
with Paris the hot core
of dreams,
was a terribly apt name
for the place I chose
to take my friend Sarah
when she had no choice
but come to New York
from her idyllic pastoral of a college
for an abortion.

From Sarah's world
of four-o'clock teas and
sit-down dinners served
with democracy by revolving
young ladies, from Sarah's world
of house mothers
named Mrs Nicely,
to a risky street
in the Manhattan
which had seduced me
as surely as the imagination
of a stroll along the Seine,
as surely as a real boy had seduced Sarah,
we came together,
but I stayed in the waiting room.

The next year
the housemothers disappeared,
along with the gentle
afternoons, and the white linen.

Now I live
on that same risky street.
The Hospital's transformed
into The French Apartments,
nice, with navy canopy,
but nothing
like the fearful sanctuary
once offered by a girl
who wanted everything
to her friend Sarah
who already knew the price.

The Cutting Edge

The girl found a new way
to do it–when they took
everything else away–
with the point
of a pencil
down her arm.

She meant to carve
'Evil,' but
the meds confused her:
She wrote it backwards.

At 5:45 pm in The Conservatory Garden

The crow comes to drink
from Pan's fountain,
which spills
into the lily pond
as the light sweetens
the day's inevitable slide
into evening, into late
August. That dark bird, out of place
amongst the lavenders
and roses, takes
off, with me
tempted to follow.

At the National Achives on Varick Street,

I find you
on microfiche-
turn, turn
the wheel, don't
want to lose you
son of Abraham and
Rebecca, child of
1920 census- "Age
eighteen, lives at home"
with all the names
of brothers and sisters,
especially my namesake,
dark, fearless, dead
Esther, your favorite,
my gift.
-"Occupation: Helper
in Poolroom"- "Place
of Birth: London," not
Vilnius, like father
Abraham, nor Massachusetts,
New World, America, like
the rest of Abraham and
Rebecca's children, you
are singular.
Now I will have you
on paper
or when I return to London, or
when I come home
to wherever you
and Esther are.

Two Days After

Finally, some sun.
From my fire escape
terrace, I look out
on another roof-
astro-turfed, lounge-chaired,
picnic-tabled, planted-
see the sculptor
spray painting his
two rectangular shapes
black.

Then, on the phone
from her farm
on the west coast
of England, Carol tells me
her daughter was all dressed
for her first Disco Night
at school, wearing the glitter
tee shirt she'd wanted, when
Carol realized
the New York skyline, the two towers
on her daughter's tiny breasts.

II.

Coming Home

Call me a circle
I re-traced the lines
Hauled and dragged years
Of lost and grasped time
To bring me dead center
With half of it owned
To bring me dead
Center   with half
of it gone

This young lady

has never forgotten
the rules: no white
after Labor Day, until
December, when it's OK.
It's winter white,
wool and pure
like the cotton white
of the gloves she wore
for appropriate occasions,
and at Dorothy Mason's
School of the Dance.

Curtsy and say "Good Evening,
Miss Mason;" wear whites
upon the court; keep
the Peter Pan collar starched
on the white blouse
of the school uniform; expect
snow by Thanksgiving; help
mother mash the potatoes;
set the table with cloth napkins;
wear a long white dress
to the Prom with the President
of the Senior Class, who later
lets his hair grow long
and white, before he decides
to take his life.

In the Blood

One Thanksgiving,
my brother told me
the willow tree
at the final bend
in the road
up the hill
to our home (now sold)
had been planted on the day he was born,
a weeping willow
on a hill of pines,
planted earlier in the day
before my father
crashed into the maple
driving home
from the hospital
from the birth of my brother
to our family tree.

529 Congress Street

Before he died,
after he knew
his son and his
partner's son
had no interest in
the store I loved
because he loved it,
he and his partner,
growing older,
agreed to sell.

The new owners failed
quickly, failed
where he had succeeded
in spinning profit
out of grace.

The store's five floors
remained vacant,
all those twenty-five
years, except for small
shoe sellers who
would come, rent
part of the ground floor,
and go.

Now there's a funky one
in the same space
the others rented,
this one called
"Terra Firma."

The Gifts

"Don't forget to turn the leaves upside down
in the water, then the lilies will draw
the moisture, and stay alive
longer," my cousin heard herself
quoting my mother to a stranger
who had just bought calla lilies.
That night I played the 78-speed
Edith Piaf records
and watched snippets
of Judy Garland movies: my mother's
favorite ladies,
which should have been a clue.
But she knew
how to keep a flower alive.

Grace

was her name, so,
of course, she had none,
as if to challenge
one more thing, our assumptions,
as she challenged us
in play-to-the-death
Scrabble or as she watched pro-football
on Sunday afternoons, while the other wives
kvetched about their husbands'
time in front of the tube,

the only mother
we knew who worked
at a profession, not a job,

who had Danish Modern furniture
in her home, always open
to those of us who craved
another model.

So when that mind began
its descent into betrayal, out
she lashed at most of us,
without grace.

Undaunted by death,
she returns in a poem,
written not to her
secret self,
rather to her way
in the world,
and how it helped
a wayward girl.

Local Talk, Wiscasset

Tide's out.

Seagull took m'clam.

Maine Coast Special's

blowin' its horn.

Hulk of The Hesper's

finally gone.

Usual traffic jam over

the Sheepscot Bridge.

Line for Red's Eats's

blockin' the street.

Long wait

for a blueberry shake.

Wild Blueberries

All year I am deprived
of them, forced, if I choose
to swallow something called "true blues,"
those silicone-injected lessons
in the evil of euphemism,
until mid-August Maine,
when wild blueberries appear
and so do I,
at every road-side stand;
like some displaced urban bear,
I lay in supplies
for my city lair,
where snow, when it appears,
stays white for only an hour.

It is a northern spirit,

pleasured by the whip
of winds, the fall
of snow, the fall
of crimson leaves,
that leave a maple
barren, except
for branches, limbs, and trunk:
sufficient, lean
and patient.

End of the Season Tour

Once Boston looked so big;
Now the MTA's a toy
train for Christmas…

Newbury Street,
Boylston: my mother
isn't taking me to shop;
my father isn't waiting for us…

Beacon Street. No more
Aunt Rose in her house
of tchotchkes. She can't
take my father to the North End or
Ruby Foo's now, or fall asleep
watching Richard Burton play *Hamlet*.
He's dead, too…

I stay with Cheryl, look
at pictures of us as
chubby children. She's
still thinner. Her mother
is withering away. Cheryl will
visit her today…

Cheryl tries to find the poem
she wrote about our fathers,
buried the same distance apart
in the cemetery
as the distance between
their desks in the office.

My brother will arrive
on New Year's Eve;
I will cry;
Cheryl's mother may die…

No swan boats
in the Public Garden, just a family
of bronze ducks on the white ground
and real ducks
in the frigid pond.

Snow clings to the trees, and
to the Ritz Carlton…

Cheryl's mother jokes
with me,
because I know
the stories…

I meet the baby, new
to Commonwealth Avenue,
his parents and my arms.
I am called "Aunt."
My sister-in-law practices
and hopes for her own…

Beacon Hill, no
memories here
where the Cabots speak
only to God. It's easy to look
in the windows. The old
lamps are lit.

III.

Rocky Mountain Prelude

In a brass bed
on a wide porch
of a blue farmhouse
in the foothills
of Longmont, Colorado,
as the sun came up
around 5 a.m.,
he told her
the little pink nightgown
would have to go…

that he'd been married
in front of a cast
of thousands, with incense
in St. Patrick's Cathedral
to a girl named Wylie
O'Hara, daughter
of a writer named John…

and this was why
she had waited
for the perfect play
to act in,
until the morning after
when he pretended
over breakfast
to have eyes only
for his hash-browns; he never
looked at her again…

but in the barn
next to the farmhouse
another enterprising lad
was brewing, stewing, stirring
teas from herbs that he had gathered,
the first teas of an empire
he would call
"Celestial Seasonings."

Cold Spring January

There's ice in the Hudson
and snow on that hill;

The wind whips
the life back;

The sun's in
the chill.

Ritual: South Florida

Every Friday, one dozen roses
to his grave, then
she gets her hair done:
in this way she worships
or she pays attention
to what matters
and what mattered,
to what serves her,
like the coiffure,
not the Sabbath candles,
this ancient little girl,
this survivor
of her saviour.

NEW ORLEANS QUARTET:
Avant et Après

Elysian Fields or
There's A Full Moon Over The Steamer Natchez

You can't go wrong
You'll get there
on the highway
with two names:
Clearview and Huey P.
Long, darlin'
the waiter will call you
at That Bar Made In Heaven,
The Napoleon House
on Chartres Street
in the city of bars, oysters and
churches: "the most religious
drunks in the world"
where the palm and tarot readers
camp outside St. Louis Cathedral
where the doors are always open
on Bourbon Street to Blues
Burlesque and Zydeco
and Jazz
is in the groin
of the beholder…

A Good Story

Civic-minded Sidney,
Alderman
of that silky city
of dexterous dichotomies
he would never
have agreed to
name "The Big Easy,"
wanted to limit
the sleazy
to one District
of Red Lights,
and Sidney Story succeeded,
beyond his tamest dreams:
a legal locality
of Devilish Dames
which bore his name,
Storyville.

*Do You Know What It Means To
Miss…New Orleans?*

Like me, New Orleans lives
with the dead:
tomb of a voodoo queen,
acres of headstones
fit for kings,
Ghost of the Quadroon Mistress
keep the Louisiana sauce
and the improvisation hot,
tumble the bougainvillaeas
over the balconies in December,
costume the Mardi Gras
revellers in February,
flow the sazeracs and
the wine of recollection
into the limbo
of our days.

New Orleans Has Collapsed!

    In Appreciation of Frank O'Hara

I was watching the hurricane news
thinking it's bad but it's not as bad
as they thought when all of a sudden
it was worse   Why??   The levees broke
and the water poured through the sexy sweet
City of New Orleans, through
cemeteries and jazz
Zydeco and oysters
booze and Blues
balconies and Brennan's
Black and White

Congregation Named Desire
Queen of the River Excess
Did the God of those Righteous Boys
now running
the U.S of A.
visit this flood upon your sensuous
banks No Noah in these Boys' plans
Oh New Orleans I love you get up !

IV.

At the American Burger

I placed a dollar bill
carefully in front of a woman
so bent over, her head
almost touched the table
at which she sat. "Excuse me;
I just wanted to give you this,"
I said before returning to the pick-up
line for my "Seattle Burger."
She picked her head up, and there
was her face, eyes so
framed by bloated puffs,
it was a surprise
to see them.
She stood up,
came over to me in line—
Behind the counter
they'd slowed down to watch—
shook her head, "No," and gave me
the dollar back.

AMERICA

Elevator Music

Alexander Calder's huge
red sculpture in Grand Rapids,
Michigan was once
so controversial
that the window of its staunchest
female supporter was shot
out by a gun.
Now its picture
is proudly printed
on the side of the city's
garbage trucks.

The Unexpurgated Activities of the Cobra Lilly

Called "Californica,"
sound and shape of erotica,
secretes honey,
seduces unsuspecting creatures
to its hollow interior,
traps them forever
in its lair of
pink and golden hair.

The Influence of Classical Music at the Metropolitan Museum

First the father,
then the mother brings
the blond baby boy in arms
as close to the pianist
as possible. The baby
kicks its legs and
looks at everything.
Who knows what he's ingested,
while the grownups
sip their wine?

*The Last Poem I Ever Want To Read Entitled
'The Last Confession'*

My father came into
my room every night
before I went
to sleep,
to kiss me, say
'Happy Face In the Morning,
Sweetheart,' then
he'd leave.

"No Problem"

Thank you
for having a nice day,
not raising
your voice or
an objection or
your hand or
a wild child;

Thank you
for acceptable noise,
ubiquitous screens,
for chat and chatter,
for more and more
and more information.

You're welcome.

ATTENTION: DANGER BEHIND

"Welcome, pick up
a veal chop and be
seated, the electric
chairs have foot
rests and are nowhere
underneath the ceiling
that leaks water and
bread. We have looked
forward to this meeting
of the minds and thighs
in hopes that the sharing
of shocks will prove to be as
productive as lightning.

Thank you
for coming and going."

Fifty years ago,

they gave her a bouquet
of roses   (remember?),
darker than the pink
of the famous stunning
suit, closer
to the color of the blood
on the famous
stunning suit (Chanel,
wasn't it?)

"She's breakin' my ass,"
he was said to have complained
about the money
she used to spend, sounding
like the Irish
tough-assed enchanter I myself
had loved, and how
could I not,
how could she not,
how could we not
have loved?

"Goodnight, David"

The Cronkite religion
was never ours:
It was that well-cast team
whose New York-
Washington play
and famous-all-over-America-
sign off
to which we were
unswervingly devoted.

Our neighbors, the only
other prodigals in our New England town
to build a "modern" house,
had a fox that came from somewhere
in the woods
to sit outside their giant picture window
at the same time every night
to watch, we all surmised,
The Huntley-Brinkley Report.

I was little, but
I knew that one was handsome
and could not understand
why I liked him
less than the one with funny ears
and the voice
my mother used to mimic
and I later came to love
as much as the short sentences,
curious cadences,
and the irony, the wit,
those much misunderstood
tools of the most humane.

Let's say,
for psychology's sake,
those early years have
all the power
we've been told.
Let's say I later
watched only political conventions that he anchored, even
switched networks when he did,
in honor of his words,
spoken in the course of one interminable
New Hampshire Primary,
"Good Heavens,
Can't we go home yet?"
Let's say
"Thank you."

"And what rough beast…?

As a well-known male poet reads on a program honoring W.B. Yeats, I watch a mascara'd, pretty, long-haired girl read *Hollywood Life*. She keeps beside her on the next chair, *Vogue*, *Town and Country*, and *American Paintings*, because the poetry is background music to the magazines. She starts to rip a subscription coupon out of *Hollywood Life*, and I explode: "Please Don't Do That!!" Another well-known poet climbs to the podium, and begins her reading with an anecdote from her college days. A professor of hers, given to drama anyway, came in one day, placed his books on the edge of the desk, and leaned over to address the class: "William Butler Yeats is dead: class dismissed."

America Enlarges Its Vocabulary Again

Now I've learned Fallujah—
I used to speak Saigon.
I know a lot of Shiite,
A little Ayatollah;

My Kandahar is better,
Better than my Bagdad.
Since I mastered Sarajevo,
I'm glad I didn't
try My Lai.

What She Learned

That it was over
when Stalin took on Hitler

What Winston Churchill meant

How 'They are bombing London' echoed
in American ears

That Roosevelt was called
Rosenstein, in Maine

A memorized list
of the American Presidents
in chronological order

That FDR stole
Norman Thomas' thunder

That people really jumped out
windows in The Depression

That Stevenson was as OK
as Eisenhower

That Calvin Coolidge said
'The more people out of work,
the more unemployment there is."

That 'enlightened Capitalism' could be discussed
with a teenage daughter

That States Rights was often an excuse
to do mean things to people

That her father never
did mean things

That history is as alive
as her father

V.

Everything Sounds So Much Better in French

One Irish-Englishman named Peter, transplanted to Brussels, speaks French, English, Flemish, Spanish, Italian, and German. He drives his French-speaking Amcrican friend whom he met in Manchester, England and his French-English-Flemish-Spanish-German-speaking son from St. Pierre Le Vieux through Cognac, Bordeaux, then left at the "HERPES" sign to "Point d'Herpes," then sees a sign for "Ball-Trap," which keeps them laughing all the way to its inevitable translation: "Clay Pigeon Shoot." They stop at seven for aperitifs.

What I Learned On My Summer Vacation In St. Pierre Le Vieux

After the first pear-fall,
bottles are tied
on the end of the branches,
the new and tiny
fruits inside, captured
to grow fat
and fill the bottles'
bottoms, to make from
trees of glass
the Eau de Vie Poire
and provoke
the question:
"How did that pear
get in there?"

The Education of Crazy Jane

When you left,
my fancy dancer, you took
words and tunes,
the talk that takes the breath away.

I had to find you
in the books:

BEFORE JOSHUAN JUDGES HAD GIVEN US NUMBERS OR
HELVITICUS COMMITTED DEUTERONOMY, I HAVE HEARD
ONE SAY THAT MEN HAVE REVERENCE FOR THEIR HOLI-
NESS AND NOT THEMSELVES, A LOT O'THRICKSTERS
SAYS I THAT WOULDN'T KNOW WHAT FREEDOM WAS IF
THEY GOT IT FROM THEIR MOTHER

Ah, the magic
that turns black
as soon as the daylight comes.

But I can tell the story
one more time.

Two Testaments

If wrestling with an angel
worked for Jacob, who had
a nasty history of trickery,
maybe it could work for you,
she offered to his lapsed Catholic
mind, forever separate
from his body, which
specialized in secret sin,
for which he could repent,
forced now to hear his own confessions,
to wrestle with the devil
who lived
in every man, particularly
in him, to wrestle even
with the particle of light manifest
in her suggestion, the closest
he would ever get
to any angel.

Brigit

It's the workin' for a woman
who would have me –
Can you believe? –
set the table for people
who were not there,
that developed such a fine
imagination in me
that I can now remember
what has never happened.

Seisun Swift, With More Than A Nod To Auden

Come for the fiddler
Take the pipe
Whip the strings
Around the gashed
    hope   bind what's still
    open   with the dance
    of mad Ireland
    that hurt
    W.B. into poetry.

THE NEWS, New Year's Eve, 1999

We watch him
light one candle, then step
outside his former prison cell,
offer the candle
to his successor
in the new South Africa.

We watch choreographed bodies
move down the corridor
past the cages
with their doors flung open,
free now
to dance on Robben Island,
to leap
beyond the flames.

Ballad Without Borders

Lawyer one day, next day vermin:
One large virus, said the German.
Not of Poland, said the Polish.
Thought you lived here? You're foolish.

He became his brother's keeper,
Walked for miles to find him
carrots, to view the sin
as it grew deeper.

Himself he kept alive
by being necessary:
Some vermin know five languages;
This made him predatory.

His liberators came
in a different uniform:
Siberia had prisons,
like the Germans: just a dorm.

Now he lives in the Florida sun,
goes to every World War II
movie that comes to town,
sits in the third row laughing,

I'm still here, you
sons of bitches,
took my kids to visit Poland
when they were old enough
       for ghosts and witches.

VI.

The Sign

There it was:
in rose, amber, palest blue.
She looked away, looked
back, and there it grew:
a perfect arc
in a cloud-puffed sky
above the wild
flowers, pebbles, shells,
above the grasses, the swell
of the waves, the recall
of Wordsworth, of *Genesis*,
of the word
she relied on: she looked
away, bent to pick
a Queen Anne's Lace, looked
up and watched each color
race from the famous unseen hand
into her open palm.

One Summer Tuesday

A fisherman and a flautist
About twelve feet apart
Stood beside the bay;

At twilight, for local color,
The flautist began to play
Greensleeves and *Red River Valley*.

The fisherman cast his line;
The evening strollers smiled
At each other;

The waves lapped, in
Alternate time.

Labor Day

The birds answer
each other or sing
what they will;
the screen door slams
by accident. The wings of
the birds flap,
like the sandled foot
hitting the wood
floor of the porch.
Even a few cars
go by. A spoon hits
the side of the bowl
in the kitchen
not far away. Later
tonight the crickets
will fight, while
the rocking chairs
stay silent.

Audubon Mots

A toast to the Masked Booby,
never tempted
to change its name
to Gavia Stellata,
the better to consort with
the Melodious Grassquit,
or failing that,
the Cuban Grassquit, able
on occasion to fly
with the American or
Caribbbean Coot,
escaping the pigeon-
hole of Greater or Lesser
White-Fronted Goose or
worse, the Eared Grebe,
Horned Grebe, or last,
the Least Grebe.

The Problem With Nature Poetry

It's possible the seagulls
knew she was worried
about picking up the big wrong
order with extra clam cakes and fries,
so when she left
for only a moment
the food in the box on the picnic
table overlooking the white masts,
about twelve of them dived
instantly into the box,
leaving only half a clam
cake and three fries. It's possible
they wanted to keep her slim,
but more likely
they were just seizing
the opportunity to do
what comes naturally.

Winter

You walk into it,
or away from it
on the road of snow;
if you could go
on beyond the "Dead
End," into
the clean
thick wood, if
you could go
into what you had
intended, or away
from it, there
would be no metaphor,
or a different one.

VII.

"Loosestrife,"

the purple calls itself,
so thick, it nearly pushes
inside the window
of the house that has stolen
her love and her money,
just a flower
in one of the gardens
she (and we) plant
with reasonable expectation
that we will continue
to delight in its flourishing,
given sufficient care,
that we will continue,
loosestrife in its place.

On the 'Island of the Old Women,'
for William Matthews

in the middle of Loch Lomond,
I wander
Inchailloch Burial Ground,
on vacation
from the year of the dead.

Whoever cared
has placed a wooden bench
for the visitor
to sit amongst the gravestones,
one from Clan MacGregor,
"family" of Rob Roy, "Celebrated
Highland Rogue," another
educated pirate.

Some gravestones offer
symbols which do honor
to the crafts
of the people buried here:
sheep, scythe, and sword,
but no symbol for a poet,
called in Scots, "makar,"
"a skilled and versatile worker
in the craft of writing."

I wish you were buried
on the "Island of the Old Women."
I wish you were buried
anywhere with a place
for words. Instead,
your incomparable talent
to disappear
at will…

Bill, tell me
if this poem's finished.

Bright Girl Wanted
for Lois

That he could stand up there, alone,
the quiet man of the pair, (she was
said to provide the flair), both,
with the long grey hair (his tied
neatly at the neck, as a doctor
would, who has long grey hair),

That he could stand up there, alone:
"Let me tell you about my wife."
(Let me tell you about my friend, his wife:
A tooth abscess spread to her brain,
infecting it.)
(That I sit here and write this.)
"Our beautiful, brilliant Mother."
That her children could stand up there, alone.
"Let me tell you about my wife:
She got her first job from *The N.Y. Times*,
An ad, you couldn't write today:

(He met her in college.)
(She went on to Columbia.)
(He went to medical school.)
(They were married for 40 years.)

"An ad, you could not write today:
'BRIGHT GIRL WANTED.'"

Taking to her bed

seemed like the province
of her wildly English
friend or of an eminent Victorian
lady, not unrelated
to her wildly English friend,
seemed seductive but a bit
indulgent to her occasional
New England self, until
the world invaded her
so fiercely
that her bed seemed the only logical
place to avoid the long knives,
defended by down, quilted,
and mauve.

My Tarot

For The King of Swords,
I read The King of Words;

For The Queen of Wands,
The Queen of Wounds.

The Ace of Wands became
The Ace of Wants.

With the suit of Cups,
I thought of "B" and "C;"

A rhyme for Pentacles:
I offered tentacles

"Guarding my heart still, but
Moving forward

Toward mastery, my secrets
With the moon."

The Club

The way a baby always
notices another baby –
That's the way I noticed
every other cripple,
permanent or temporary, after
my leg was wrapped in bandages,
so only I could see the gash.

Or the way they noticed me,
stared at one wrapped leg and
one tanned leg, both defiant,
sticking out there
under my short skirt: the woman
with metal crutches, the man
who could barely fit his wheelchair on the bus,
and the driver who had to wait.

2001

Amputations are in
this year: two towers,
one brother, my money,
even some teeth:
burning gaps
like the severing
of my mother's leg
just below the knee,
not a metaphor,
just the first amputation,
which should have prepared me

No Cain and Abel
for Paul

It's just us now
and I'd say we'd seen
everything together,
but family stories vary, like
eye-witness accounts
at scenes of accidents or crimes.

Did we have the same
father and mother?
Do the years between us
approximate the time difference
between our two coasts?

You're so blond.

We keep our distance,
except when we don't,
and we don't go farther away
than the three thousand
miles of our careful map.

You're left-handed.

We both had baseball
gloves; we both played
poker; we ran away
from home; we came back
with divergent levels
of tolerance for horror.

You found safety
sooner. For you
there is no question: "Am I
my sister's keeper?"
I get to steal the question and
ask it whenever I please.

"And that has made all the difference"

When Robert Mitchum and Jimmy Stewart
died within one day of each other
it became clear
that every choice or accident
had brought me to this
moment of unavoidable recognition
that the world was divided
between Robert Mitchum people
and Jimmy Stewart people
and I was Robert Mitchum people
and I'd been having one hell
of a wonderful life.

Sleep, why
should anyone go to:

sleep, that
knits up the raveled sleeve
of care,
which Macbeth does murder,
through which his Lady walks
with miles to go

sleep, per chance
to dream

die, to sleep
no more

Like a 'rest' in music,

               but
there is no rest:
It hits you
in the bathtub on a Friday afternoon,
not the calendar
marked for memory
that you prepare for
in vain, like the preparation
for the original death.
The water's song runs over the parts
of your body that
are left.

Dialogue

Come, dearest, we'll play
A little poker,
Stud and Draw,
The first game you taught me.
I'll bring our plastic chips;
You'll win; I'll take
Your hand; I'll take
You out of here.
Listen, I'm pretending
I can talk to you.
Pretend you can
Hear me.
Come, dearest,
Come back.

When my poem appeared

in a respected and established
national and international magazine
that people could actually buy
on newsstands,
people used the word
"proud," as in, they were
of me,
as if I had
the baby,
enough money,
made peace in the Middle East
and Northern Ireland,
stabbed a stake through
the heart of racism,
wrested power from the badguys
who didn't deserve it,
sat beside my father through
the moment of death,
found a lover who fought
to keep me;
and when my poem appeared,
I had.

Sprezzatura
for W.M

Say he cultivated it,
then watch
the innocence smolder
to experience,
the laughter
to irony,
the shadows deepen,
the steps missed,
the heart crack wider,
the touch
stay light.

Photograph © Michael Ian

ESTHA WEINER is co-editor and contributor to *Blues For Bill: A Tribute To William Matthews* (Akron Poetry Series, 2005), and author of *The Mistress Manuscript* (Book Works, 2009) and *Transfiguration Begins At Home* (Tiger Bark Press, 2009). Her poems have appeared in numerous anthologies and magazines, including *The New Republic* and *Barrow Street*. Nominated for a 2008 Pushcart Prize, she was a 2005 winner of a Paterson Poetry Prize, and a 2008 Visiting Scholar at The Shakespeare Institute, Stratford, England. Estha is founding director of Sarah Lawrence College NY Writers' Nights Series, Marymount Writers Nights, and a Speaker on Shakespeare for The New York Council For The Humanities. She is a Professor in the English Dept. at City College of NY, and serves or has served on the Poetry/Writing faculties of The Frost Place, The Hudson Valley Writers' Center, Stonecoast Writers' Conference, Poets and Writers, Poets House, and The Writer's Voice. She also serves on the Advisory Board of Slapering Hol Press, Hudson Valley Writers Center. In her previous life, Estha was an actor and worked for BBC radio.